Sticky Notes

Kylie Nelson

Presentation by *BookLeaf Publishing*

Web: www.bookleafpub.com

E-mail: info@bookleafpub.com

ISBN : 9789357449120

First edition 2021

To My Mom

To my mom
For showing me that strength
Is sometimes running as far as you can
For reminding me
That all you can do is laugh and move on
For teaching me
To look at the bigger picture,
It is easier to see the red flags when you aren't
using them as blindfolds
For letting me be your first love,
You always be mine as well.

Karma

Karma
I believe in Karma
I have faith that the universe
Will take care of you for me
And I hope it sucks for you

I

You will cry
Not once
Not twice
Not even thrice
Until the tears
Tear open
Every piece of hurt
From the moment the words slip
Right from your lips
It will sting like a whip
Sleep will be a sweet mercy
To all the pain you will feel
But my darling, you will heal.

Grief

I know grief
Like an old friend
You only see a few times a year.
I have practiced goodbye
Rehearsed all those lines
Making sure I hit all the right cues.
I can identify the ten stages
Within my self
And within others.
On a scale of one to ten
I'll point to my heart
It is a fifteen right here doc.
I know grief
Like an old friend
I learned to greet at the door.

You Can't

You can't call me that anymore,
As if I'm still yours.
You can't text me with the jokes we made
Like we weren't just fighting at 3:36 am.
You can't come around randomly
As if you haven't left me seventeen times
before.
You can't ask me if I'm okay, or how my day
was
Like you caring now will suddenly change the
fact that you didn't before.
You can't say hello
As if you'll be here when I remind myself why I
said goodbye.
You can't ask me if I'm busy
Like there wasn't a time my world revolved
around you.
And you can't make me the bad guy
As if the blood didn't cover just mine, but yours
too.

Parallel

I think, maybe
There is a parallel universe
Where we never crossed paths
You never got to know me
My world did not revolve around you
My heart never broke
You never said those words
Oh, what a universe that would be
For you to have never met me.

Red Flags

Red flags are easy to miss
When you use them as blindfolds
Cover them in shiny things
Wearing rose coloured glasses

One Day

One day this will all be a dull ache
It will not affect me like it does now
It will not haunt my every moment.
One day
I will be able to stand proud and bow
I will not seek your approving comments.
One day
I will be able to hear your name
And not try to run in the opposite direction.
One day
This will not hurt the same
You won't mean a sliver of a fraction.
One day
I will heal from you
Like everything else.
One day
You will hold no power over me
What a great day that will be.

Starting Over

You can start over
That is okay
You can nearly be at the end
And decide to turn around
There is no shame in that.
You can start over
It doesn't have to be today
It doesn't have to be tomorrow
It doesn't even have to be this year or the next.
You, and only you
Get to decide
When to start over
Why you'll start over
How you're going to start over
And where you will start over.
But you can
Now,
Or later,
Or never.
You can.

I learned

And somewhere
I learned
Who I am.
Without your expectations,
Without the cage you had built
Holding me captive
Refusing me growth.
I stole the keys
I shattered every last one of those bars
And somewhere
I bloomed
Into who I am today.

Bloomed

The girl who is free
Is not same one you knew
Because she grew
Into everything she was
Ever made to be.

The Beauty In It

There is beauty in it.
It is incredibly messy,
It is not to be romanticized,
Nonetheless there is beauty in it.
Finding pieces of yourself
As the sunrises after a restless night
At the river where you soothe your battered soul
In the pages of someone else's words
In making your bed for the first time in a long
time
As you take the long way around
In the singing of your favourite song carefree
again.
Healing is perhaps the messiest thing you'll ever
do
But there is strength there as well,
And that makes it beautiful.

II

Heal.
Cry when you hear that song.
Heal.
Laugh at the awkward moments.
Heal.
Get angry at those who pretend to have known.
Heal.
Curse their name for leaving.
Heal.
Allow yourself to feel,
Allow yourself to heal.

III

As a child
I helped my grandma in her garden
We would dead head all the flowers
We did it so that the new ones could grow
In order to replace the spaces
We had to take the bad away.
As a child
I was told picking up litter
Made the Earth heal
As if it was only a splinter
In the Earths thumb.
My fingers stained
In flower dye
Garbage junk
Messy; it is messy to heal
Work; it is work to heal
Beautiful; it is beautiful to heal.

Allowance

You are allowed to get lost
You are allowed to lose something
You are allowed to hurt
You are allowed to feel things
So deeply the world could stop in motion.

You are allowed to make mistakes
You are allowed let the world fall short
You are allowed to scream
You are allowed to curse
Until it feels like you can't anymore.

All of that makes you human
All of that hurts
But in order to heal,
It must all hurt first.

IV

I had told myself
I would not let anyone close to me m
So close it would hurt if they left
But you took every wall I built
And removed it
Brick by brick
But you sat in my silence
Telling me you'd wait forever
Minute by minute
But you killed the distance
And moved in
Inch by inch
And you stayed

Outlier

Love did not stay
It has a history of leaving
Right when I needed it the most

Love has not been kind
Love has been cruel and punishing
Love has filled me up, just to leave me

But you
You have stayed
Despite all my fears of you leaving too
You have been kind
A sweet taste I am not used to
You have been patient
There is no coaxing, you'd rather wait for me
You are completely different than any type of
love I have ever know.

Come Inside

If you come inside
Do not mind the mess at the door
I am still getting rid of all those from before
Watch your step for the baggage
I am still learning how to let go
Mind your feet for splinters
I am still perfecting the imperfect
Don't worry about the cracks in the windows
I am learning to let the light in
Be careful to stay close
It is easy to get lost in the twists and turns
Be sure to bring a jacket
I am still learning how to not get cold

No Need

You do not need to heal me
I am not shattered
I am not broken
I am not lost
You do not need to heal me
I will do that on my own
I will pick up my own pieces
I will mend what is hurting
I will find my own path
You do not need to heal me
But darling,
It would be nice to hold your hand

V

I wrote poems on sticky notes
After ripping off a bandaid
Cutting open a scar.

I whispered 'I hate you' in a mirror
And found found peace
In the silence that came after.

I talked until midnight
Trying to force myself to sleep
Joking about 0/10 i would never do this again.

I busied myself with work or school
As my heart hurt
Convincing myself I could deal with this pain
after.

But I wrote poems on sticky notes
And I let the gapping wound heal to a scab.

For you

Dear you,
You. The one reading this.
I hope you find peace, in whatever way matters.
One day your heart will not hurt.
Not like this anyways.
I hope you know you are enough.
Remind yourself of it.
Scream it on the top of your lungs because you
are.
You are enough.
I may not know many things,
But this much I know.
I hope you let the light in.
Even if it is a bit blinding.
I hope you find whatever you need to find.
Now, later and always.
I hope no matter what you keep searching for the
beauty in things.
It is easy to constantly see the mess.
Don't stop searching.

Sincerely,
Me.

www.ingramcontent.com/pod-product-compliance
Lightning Source LLC
Chambersburg PA
CBHW070738160726
48003CB00006BA/2560